THE PROMISED CHILD

DAVID IS THE NAME

RICK HUTCHINS

The Promised Child
Copyright © 2022 by Rick Hutchins

ISBN
978-1-958122-34-1 (Paperback)
978-1-958122-33-4 (eBook)
978-1-958122-35-8 (Hardcover)

CONTENTS

RENSEY IS THE NAME!

I thank God for helping me write this book. Everything come from him very much. He knows my mind well as my heart. I was born (Rensey L. Hutchins) sometimes called Mr. Ricky. Early August of '66 my mother bare me. In a town called Dayton, Ohio. Which is North of Cincinnati, South of Toledo. Dayton the boom town, when you hear/say. You probably! Would think of a city like Vegas. Where manufactory was if. Now a city like purgatory and distress. I was raised a bit in the projects called Desoto Bass in the 1970's. Where living was comfortable. Not like now. The second child of six sibling. A single mother with welfare and no help from the fathers. It's like I came from a dysfunctional family pretty much. But God blessed me to be a leader to my family. People in General looks up to me for understanding as wisdom. If the lord can take criticism/pain on the cross. I can take life and be content. Growing up is a pained. Where I never had anything until the God above gave until me.I had the nerves and money was quite tasteful.until the lord took it from me.Then I knew, never to take life for granted. I moved to Aurora Colorado in the mid-80's. I love the mountains, lakes & people. But most of the time I stayed sick. Well! My body wasn't used to the elevation of the state. Sinus congestion/ears pluge was very <u>miserable</u> to me. I was there a good 3 month tops. Until I made up my mind to move back to Ohio. Which was an insult to me. I think of myself less of a person more than life it's self. I put myself last so I can be first later on. Let me tell you something also at the Lord God. He has brought me from a distance.

From living place to place. Staying with people that didn't care about you. All they wanted was there money first of the months. Fornication with women's that didn't have a handle on life. One time! I remember when I was 16 years of age I wanted to be a rich man. I didn't know how to be. But I was ready to make a change in my nothing for good life of minds. It started 1983 when I told my mom standing in the kitchen of the house. That one day, I would be rich. She said, Oh son! Don't forget about Momma. I giggle hard. I was in high school at Dunbar High that sat on Richley Dr. (Formerly). Now that it sit closes to Nicholas Rd. It's was great times in that era. Wild characters in school the 80's was less dramatic then any other time/era. Great guy's/beautiful girls/teachers. Only a young man like me can imagine in <u>dreams</u> of <u>course</u>. I was sure of shy but had a temper to reckon with. Which I sort of grown out of over the years of maturity. Like a man that strike <u>gold</u>. My high school counselor for <u>O W E</u> found me a job at <u>Frisch's</u> Downtown Main St. as a dishwasher in the basement of the restaurant. I like going to work in the afternoons. Because, I needed 3 credits to graduate for the requirement. At the times I still smell the aroma of the cook's cooking in the kitchen when walking to the back to go to the restaurant basement. I couldn't wait to get off work for my usual, that was a Hot Big Boy with extra sauce, loaded with lettuce and pickle. No cheese. And fresh hot French fries and warm apple pie. And a cold glass of root beer. To me alone. That's was great eating to me. While thinking about life and what was in stored for me. After high school. I worked for Arby's.

Burger King in '85. Then '86 I worked for McDonald's where I started a short-term career in management. Where I learned a lot on a business scaled. On how to manage people, money, inventory and computer skills. I notice I started developing weight for working there. Because, I would eat after work. Go to work starving and leave work filled. I was with McDonald's for five years after I moved back from <u>Colorado</u>. I worked at the Wilmington Pike Store for two and half years. Then I left to take a job at Auto Works parts store in the West Town Center on 3rd St. I was there 4mos tops and hated it. So, I left to go back to McDonald's on Keowee Ave to work there for 5 years max. Then I knew that I was getting fed up with fastfood period. Then I left for good that time to work for the Marriott

Hotel on Patterson Blvd. Where my dreams was a sure. In '91 I was a Hotel Associate where I made lot of money. From <u>Bellman</u>, and <u>Banquet Server</u>. I wore many hats in there. For five years I was growing to succeed in life. With each job I was tipped. For getting to mention Housekeeping Houseman I was in change to take linen to Housekeeper's Carts. Believe it or not! I met famous individual's working there. I really pursuit happiness with that line of work. Where you are very interactive with everyone you would come in contact with. It was a great place to work and meet great people for sure. Where learning how to make up a bed from carrying luggage for guest to making a drink for a guest to folding a towel for health club member to clearing a table off for a guest in the restaurant. I did it all except management. That's when I knew for a man my caliber/color no advancement for me at all. Upper management love to see me there working. But me over somebody was forbidden for a black man to manage or supervise a department. I had to keep telling myself I need my own business where I'm in charge of things. You see years prior to that someone has told me, that I need my own business, that I would make a great boss. But seeing is believing.

So! I thought about it quite often about being a entrepreneur in this lifetime. But didn't realize it was really hard to start.

But I didn't care because, soon or later! I will have a business. I sat out to put my plans in motion. But God had other plans for me. Beside, he was in control of my life and everything else. God gave me a little lead way. Here is how he did it. I moved out of my mother/stepfather house in '91 to a one bedroom apartment in Timber Creek off of Cornell Dr. My rent was $385.00 a month. I still couldn't keep up. Because, McDonald's was paying every two week (Twice a month). I hated it. So! I got served a eviction notice one day for being delinquent on my rent. Enough was enough! So! I moved out without notice on a weekend. Heck! With that! I moved in with a man name <u>Sidney</u> <u>Rey</u> who taught me a lot of thing about today society. And I was learning for what its worth. I thing that was important was living/ money which both go hand in hand. And I learned everything there was about it, well! When I moved in, I stay in the basement of his house. I I left McDonald's in '91. And reported to Marriott two weeks later. Well! At the Marriott I got paid every-week on a Thursday's man! I started putting forth and effort in saving money. I remember one day I had a vicious toothache where I wouldn't go to the dentist. Because, it would cost me a money. So! I took Advil and went on to work. I was consider a penny pincher. By '92 I made my first <u>$10,000.00</u> by sticking to my plan. Every week I was saving money like the government taken it from you. I would paid my rent then paid myself $30.00 and the rest went to the bank. I went and invested in a <u>IRA</u> for retirement and by <u>3 mutual funds</u> all 3 funds had $2,500.00 in them. Man! I was on my way with success/ dreams. '93 I let my car go and started walking to work for health.

I didn't have a lot of weight on me. But building my vascular system by walking to work for a good solid 2½ years. Did me some good actually a lot of good. Rain, sleet, snow, thunder/lightening I walk. I live at 2316 Germantown St. walk down to Stewart St. a straight shot to the hotel on Stewart/Patterson. I was eager to get to work. At the time all I could think about is making money. And believe me! I was making it for sure. Indeed.My Lord and Savior he has kept me safe. From harm/danger. I thank God for keeping me. I didn't realize it unto later years. That's when it hit me. That God was in control of my life. And not me.

There was times I can relate to King David, Joseph, Jeremiah, and John. On how God used these men of the biblical times. Forgotten! to mention prophet job. Who is a lesson to all of us, where a man didn't believe in sin and stayed faithful to God regardless how Satan came at him. Paul! Once told me to be content with life as it came at you. Wow! A man that murder Christians. Telling me to be contend with life? This is hard to swallowed. A man that changed from worst to greatness for the lord sake. Where I can relate to that to. Me! A changed man at heart. Where I turned from a life of sin. And turned to God before destruction happen to me. Oh! Yes! My life was on a downward spiral. Believe me! Not nothing <u>humorous about it.</u> The world/sin can tare your life apart if you let it. With Jesus! In my life now. I can accomplished life as a gourmet chef with a great recipes for living Ok! Doing and knowing the word of God. Is sweet to the soul.

WEAKER VESSEL IS A DISTRACTION

It was 1996 when life for me was kind to me a minute or so. I had gotten my first home on Iola Ave. I moved out from Sidney Rey house on Germantown St. and Iola Ave. I was doing big things in my life. A two bedroom home w/ car garage nice basement, family room and small kitchen. I was big time, little that I knew was a pain for being on my own. I learned quickly for being a homeowner. I had to fixed it out of pocket expense. Wow! did I catch on. One evening after work. I decided to cut my grass. When Ismae! A beautiful girl from the Bahamas stays and talk to me. Actually! She stop to talk everyday with me. We got use to each other company. Until her cousin Rossalyn show up at my door. She was Satan in a dress. Waiting for the right moment to in tice/seduce me. She was there for the break up our friendship. And she did do the job she was set out to do. So! Ishmae stop coming over. Because, Rossalyn ended up with me. I really like Ishmae alot.

But Rossalyn was very persuasive. But our relationship was short live. Because, God don't like <u>ugliness</u>. We <u>fornicate</u> until it became sicking to the soul. And death was waiting on both of us if we didn't stop. I got rid of her quickly out my life once and for all. At the time I wasn't as close to God then I should of being. I should of known better to let a women like her in my life. Oh well! I had to bump my big heads hard, for understanding. A weaker vessel with distraction at hand. (Her body). King David was a lesson with Bathsheba. It's sees that a beautiful woman can cause a downfall for a man if mess with.

In high school I was called the <u>ass man</u>. Because, I loved a girl with a big butt and hips. That was my kind of lady. Somehoww, some way I could persuade them in to having sex. And I did. She would make me a happy boy the women I was intange with was Wanda C., Tersina S., Dionne R., Dionne E., Michelle B., Charlene F., Linda T., Tammy J., Rossalyn J., Jamie M. So! Man/boys alike beauty is only skin deep. I should of look at the heart of a female. Instead of her outward appearance. A great heart, a great mind and focus on the prize of Jesus. As you see these are elogence times meaning things are nice in a way people put them. But vulnerable to innocent one's with no retroelect to life.

NOT MY
FATHER'S
KEEPER

When I was a youngster. I kinda knew something was wrong in the picture. My mother was there and brother and sisters. But one thing was funny for sure. Was my father absents (MIA) a lot. He was never around us. Let the truth be known about these coward, low life, no good of a man never did anything for us. I didn't know who he was until my mom mention him sitting in a truck with a friend of his. She said, that's your father! Huh! was my reaction. I try my hardest to let this man in my life. But at times it's seems that we are on two different path's. I say to myself that this can't be right. I see he put money before his offspring's. <u>Ashamed</u> <u>Huh</u>? I know men that would put their job before God/ family. I try to look at women's behavior before I approach them. Because, their way of life. Alot of them can't get a handle on life. Man! Just as bad as woman with life. I was with Linda T. for a long time. We respected each other. We enjoyed each other's company. But she had nasty intolerable differences for as smoking weed/drinking. Not my kind of lady. Truth be known. I enjoyed the fornication with her as well as she did with me. We were unseparational. Like a saddle on a horse. Until one day I realize that I couldn't do it no more. She was separated from her husband at the time. And I didn't care at the time. But the Lord God, show me something in a dream. I told Linda T. no more of me/her. After what God has showed me. I come to my senses. What he showed me was going to take my life if I wouldn't stop doing and listen to him. Like Samuel told Saul its better to obey than to sacrifice. The Devil has plans for me to. But he lose to God way. But I sometimes think that I need a good-looking woman at my side. But I don't. I need a God-fearing woman with. Their everyday life takes a lose. When you leave God out! Believe me your life is messed up. Like his! Example! His family tree is short. He's has no biological grandkids but two, the grandson that's it. From me its punishment. From God sake, its a <u>cursed</u>. For mis-treated of your offsprings. Believe it or not! <u>I</u> <u>Rensey</u> is very gifted. I'am a promise child to my mother. My father father name me. Knowingly I was planeted in the middle of their lives. I believe that God has a purpose for us when we are born. Life is only how you choose it. I do believe that the bible is truth to every word that is written. As <u>Christ we shouldn't live by bread alone</u>. That's was well said, Don't live or take life alone. The Bible is a great recipe for living. It was the 25th of July 2015. I was sitting and thinking how <u>God</u> has brought me a mighty long way of faith. I never forget as long as the creator keeps me.

HUMILITY/
INTEGRITY

As a man of God. I have to have humility not pride. I need <u>integrity</u> not <u>frustration</u>. I need love and hope. Not hate and envy. Put forth good and wise not evil and discouragement. I do honour and respect. Smile more. Less frowns. And I have accepted life for what it's worth, this is what I said, about life.

Life is my wife. She can be beautiful if she wanna. She can be a pain, when thing's are let be. When you don't worried about a thing. That when she is good and at her best. You can be intrigue by the thing's she offer in her. Don't touch her and not to be unexpected to be <u>harm</u> you play and he burn. You slack and lose. You love and learned. Faith and hope I will choose.

You see! God has giving me life as a wife I divorce her when its over on earth.

EYE'S OF COLORS

I was called a N_ _ _ _R once before to my face. Because of a friendship with a decent woman/husband. I was shooked by the gay's tone of voice instead of the name calling. He later apologize for the behavior of course his job was on the line. Weeks later he die from a car accident. I saw a man that was unfit for society. He made some bad decisions/with wrong choices. He don't care! He live life as it would expected him to live. You see, by 1993 I had more friends Black/White than I had money with problem. I accepted them all like Christ accepted us in God's family. God himself made me a great leader to be. Because, I do play servant all the times. That I work for other people. Which I know we all work for the lord God's glory/will. If we save the eye's of colors we would all be mislead in life. I know there is a difference in being a true brother then a nigger. 1) a brother will feed you the word of God then to cursed you out. 2) He would ask to see if you are ok. 3) He would be the one to feed God's sheep. Now on the other hand a - feed you some street knowledge about a gun. 3) He would care about he's wheels $5,000.00 on $1,500 car. Oh! Now their is a difference in desent white people. Then the ignorant whites. 1) Desent whites would come and befriend you. 2) They would cry/hurt when you suffer. 3) They would offer help in any situation and problem. Now ignorant white's 1) They would let the prejudice speak for them. 2) Feed you twins evil/hate. 3) Hold on to the past than to let go. And grab the future hope/love.

THE BORN AUTHORITY

When you know that you are first in everything. That's when you are a leading person. I know for sure the ego system do work for me. I was born to lead. I may be nothing. But God create something out of nothing. That's me! Let's look at what I mean. For example my bosses work for me. No words spoken, and they take care of me. My money is on time, they do make sure that my family/I are eating. You fired them by leaving the company. They are stressed over big issueses. I on the other hand is on vacation relaxed free of stress. So! They work for me. I work for the lord God. In reality! Your employer is the employee. I see the system in another way. The government runs the country. In reality the Riched runs the country. If no one wouldn't pay taxes the county would go broken. The (Riched) Banks took over. Without our money in the bank's. The bank's again will lose. They need our money to make money. So! The government and corporation of American go hand in glove together. I see it 365 day's a year. Ashamed right? You/I can't keep up. Because the government and companies don't want you/I to get ahead of things to them. They give you/I enough to functions. Taxes is illegal! But the scam is the system. The system is made up of people who think they are the powers to be. As showed enough as my shoes are <u>run over and ugly</u>. That's the government sloppy/ugly! I see more ties/then tattoos. Crooks then straighten way's.

There is no greater authority then the one true God of Heaven/earth. Remember that.

LIFE'S
DONUT'S

When I was just 5 yrs. old. I love life which I didn't know any better. Too! Much life is not good for you. It can be very unhealthy for you. If you don't know. I see people of all walks of life. I see the world is made up of different flavors. And the earth is the case that holds everything in it. Good ones, bad ones, stale ones, soft ones, and hard ones, which holds two of life ingredients <u>Rich/ Poor</u>. Big Boy came to order the whole case. Now that's some glutton for you. He's mission is to stay fat. (Government). Everyday life's cycles is sound with a hole in it. And I try not to fall in it. (Worst habits, God situation, Hate/Evil problems, greed/ lust, and envy/malice). This are the artificial ingredients that counter act with life's donuts (people)

GOD'S PROMISE TO A CHILD!

I know God's way is righteousness then my way. My way is diluted with sin/ Tyranny of the world. I found my God and lord and saviour Jesus Christ which found me. But when the world is so wicked at times. Humbleness is the least you see. The sin is so great. It's like syrup, think and potent of evil. But God's promise is to the child who is <u>obedient</u>, humble, show mercy, and keep his words at heart. I will remain at his side. God has giving me a couple of #'s <u>3</u> and <u>7</u>. This #'s belong to the child who know him, the promise will stand when everything else will perish without doubt. God's promise is here. Sin is running rampage. Pride walketh in front of you and death is two steps behind you. I notice that every day, hour and minutes. We are granitite toward destruction. That's when sin has run its course. I'am the Promise Child that God had in mind. (Rensey is the name)

www.ingramcontent.com/pod-product-compliance
Lightning Source LLC
Chambersburg PA
CBHW031234120626
46545CB00003B/1116